DON MEE CHOI

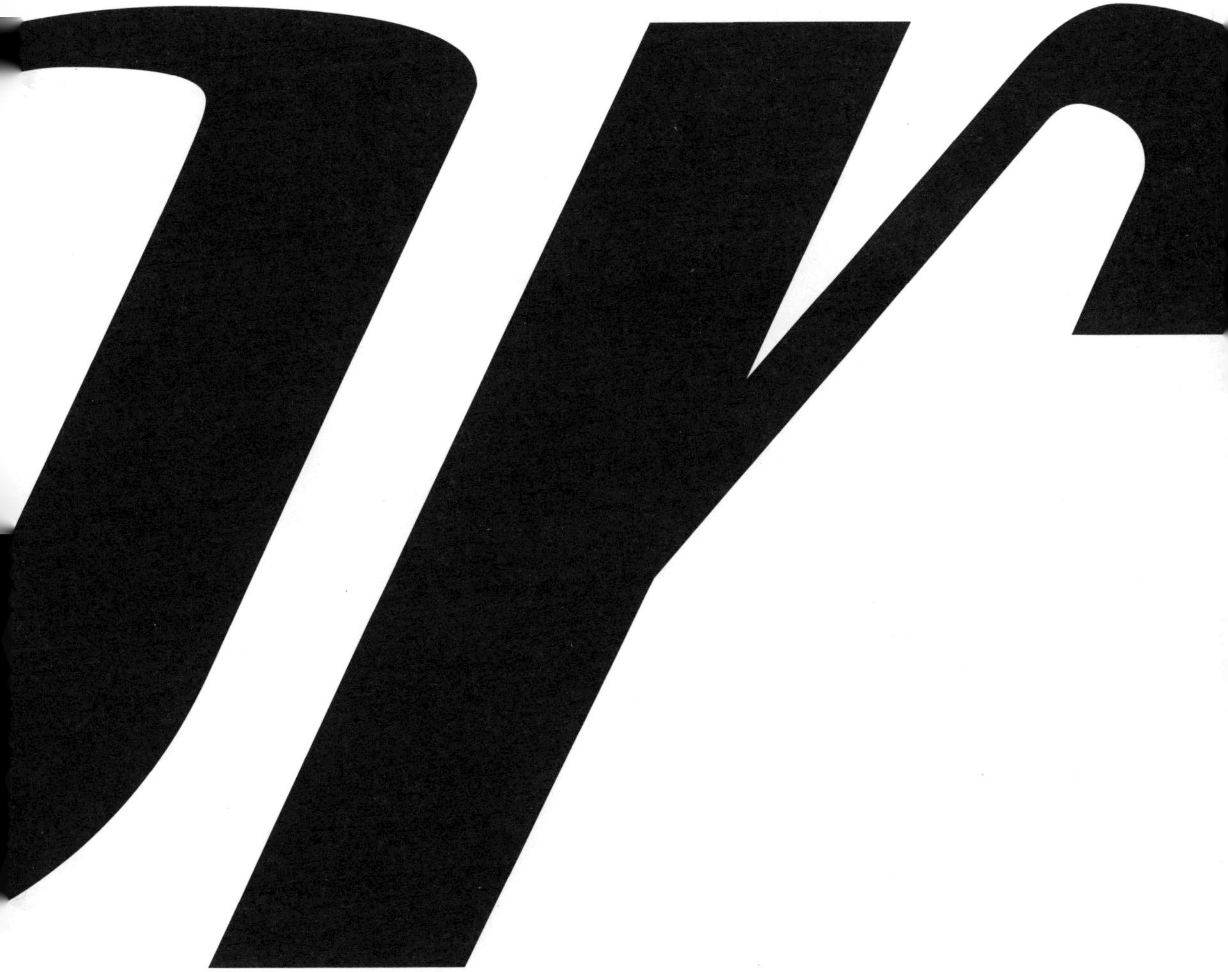

WAVE BOOKS / SEATTLE & NEW YORK

Published by Wave Books

www.wavepoetry.com

Wave Books titles are distributed to the trade by

Consortium Book Sales and Distribution

Phone: 800-283-3572 / SAN 631-760X

Library of Congress Cataloging-in-Publication Data

Names: Choi, Don Mee, author.

Title: Mirror nation / Don Mee Choi.

Description: First edition. | Seattle : Wave Books, 2024.

Identifiers: LCCN 2023041551

ISBN 9798891060005 (hardcover)

ISBN 9781950268931 (paperback)

Subjects: LCGFT: Essays. | Poetry.

Classification: LCC PS3603.H65 M57 2024 | DDC 811/.6—dc23/eng/20230919

LC record available at https://lccn.loc.gov/2023041551

Designed by Crisis

Printed in Canada

9 8 7 6 5 4 3 2 1

First Edition

Wave Books 114

Most people are principally aware of one culture, one setting, one home; exiles are aware of at least two, and this plurality of vision gives rise to an awareness of simultaneous dimensions, an awareness that—to borrow a phrase from music—is contrapuntal.

—Edward W. Said, *Reflections on Exile and Other Essays*

I drive language on, all the way into the worst pun (which is something I am always accused of), so that language has to say the truth, even against its will.

—Elfriede Jelinek, *Sports Play*

Evidently all angels are spheres. And bizarre, to the extent that they manifest as snow.

—Alexander Kluge, *The Snows of Venice*

MIRROR NATION

BERLIN 28.6.2019

The westerly wind blows across a patch of desert outside my apartment window facing north: the Deutschlandradio, the ever-spinning ring of Mercedes-Benz, and the metal fences set up for the construction of new housing. Only the fences remind me of home— the endless barbed wire across the waist of a nation. A cooler temperature expected this morning before the heat wave arrives tomorrow. On 28.6.1950, in Seoul, three days after the war had begun, my father washed his face and looked up at the stars on a clear night, then decided to head out to the city center. Photos of the war had yet to appear in the nation's newspapers. No one was on the road. The East Gate was still standing, but the police station was empty. The tracks shone under the stars but there were no trams to be seen. I merely merrily washed my face and looked out to the ring of Benz lit at dawn, and finally caught a strand of remote signal from my father. V6. *V* frequently stands for *violence* and *virtue*. An understatement, perhaps. I didn't know what to make of 6, except that 6 persists as June, and that it comes after number 5, which has been discreetly established as 5=O in a glossary of translingual puns. As my father did seventy years ago to his unborn daughter, I channeled into the most remote canyons of the desert—Are you OK, ROK? I'm childless, so I have no choice but to channel into the desert of memory.

In my future city of two Koreas, I began reliving the acute feelings of separation from home. I would shake them off by midmorning by pacing in my spacious apartment, then they'd return again the following day. The incessant chirping of the sparrows perched on tall birch trees outside my balcony only heightened my grief. This inexplicable ailment, which began in Hong Kong when we left South Korea during the dictatorship, had magnified over the years, then it had somewhat subsided the past twenty years as I settled, often numbing myself with work involving translation after translation. The unexpected return of my childhood grief prompted me to search for the remote waves of my father, my other universe. The ring of Benz was a radar of some sort. Like a compass, it operated magnetically and, not surprisingly, it also had a capacity for sonic sensitivity. It didn't take me long to detect the exact location. I spotted my father on a bridge, once again. This time he was standing on Glienicker Brücke, between Berlin and Potsdam. The fate of Korea's waist was decided at the 1945 Potsdam Conference, by Churchill, Stalin, and Truman. From where I stand, facing north, the geopolitics of division have long been eroded by incessant wind—vanished or buried beneath the sand. Korea's waist remains fatefully inconsequential. My father waved to me across a vast distance, from his present dimension: We are still not OK!

POTSDAM 11.2.1986

On 11 February 1986, the last spy swap takes place on Glienicke Bridge, connecting Berlin and Potsdam. What is unique about this spy swap is that it is also the first to happen in public. Interpreted as a sign of thawing relations between East and West, the event on what will now forever be known as the Bridge of Spies plays out in front of the world's press.

(Rundfunk Berlin–Brandenburg)

A bitterly cold morning, my father recalled. I tracked his white hat with earflaps quickly receding into the sea of cameras. There were swans under the bridge on the Havel that morning. They also receded quietly, paddling between the broken sheets of ice, without being noted by the world. As always, S stands for *spy* and *swap*. Obviously, swans have nothing to do with S. Occasionally, S stands for *sympathy* or *symphony*, and also goes undetected.

Sometimes, the flow of time is reversed for no apparent reason, and goes undetected even by the ring of Benz, which has been observed to spin in only one direction—clockwise. How my father's white hat with earflaps blew in closer and closer like a balloon was a mystery even to me. The only logical conclusion I have arrived at is that one's childhood ailment can create havoc in the magnetic field of memory. Although there are incidents where time neither moves clockwise nor counterclockwise. It remains paralyzed as if in a stupor, as it was in the case of the clock in Shōhei Imamura's film *Black Rain*. The time on the clock is almost 08:15, the time of the atomic bombing of Hiroshima. Time utterly destroyed.

But its surviving double keeps returning throughout the film as an old-fashioned, chiming clock. Its minute hand has to be repeatedly reset to the beeping sound of the seven o'clock news on the radio. (The radio and the ring—they may be twins.) The missing hour, the impending doom, persists like the dark spots on the faces and arms of the survivors. Clumps of hair fall out due to radiation sickness. Hairy hell. Everyone might as well be dead, and that is exactly what the deferred hour—eight o'clock—signals, that they're already dead and will die again, chime again. Handless.

And what to make of the numbers 681945, though I can't say for certain that they always follow after *V*, as there are many other numerations of atrocities, orbiting history's magnetic field. But what I can say is that this particular set was so finitely determined that it might as well have been an amalgamation of pure negativity, which has never been fully repented for by its implementers, ever. That said, the missing hour may serve as sufficient evidence that trauma has a tendency to create havoc on memory. This may also explain why *S* will have nothing to do with *T*, which, as we all know, stands for *terror* or *tanks*. So be it. Stupor or torpor.

BRIDGES OF =

I was overwhelmed by the silent lament of the angels, who have kept their station above our endless calamities for nigh on seven centuries. Their lament resounded in the very silence of the chapel and their eyebrows were drawn so far together in their grief that one might have supposed them blindfolded.

(W. G. Sebald, *Vertigo*)

= TAEDONG BRIDGE = GLIENICKER BRÜCKE = HANGANG BRIDGE =

= SWAN = EISERNER STEG = LANGENSCHEIDTBRÜCKE =

The house I was born in was near the Hangang Bridge. On June 28, 1950, the bridge was blasted by the South Korean Army to deter the advancing North Korean troops. Many refugees fleeing the city fell to their deaths as the bridge collapsed. Our house is no longer there, but it persists in my memory. It speaks to me in a language only the homesick understand. My mother tells me that, as soon as I could walk, I reveled, walking on the bridge. I grew up listening to the rippling laments of the bridge. As children, my sister and I believed that angels flew down from the sky to bathe inside the hollow legs of the bridge. The angels sang as they bathed. That's how we knew they were inside the legs. Sometimes, we waited till dusk on the sandbank, where we played, to catch a glimpse of the departing angels.

Before I was born, when my mother was pregnant with my older brother, she dipped into Han River and floated about. She was not exactly a swan, but she might as well have been because she looked so happy then, her eyebrows drawn so far apart. I must repeat that swans have nothing to do with *S* or with *T*, for that matter. I think of Taedong Bridge in Pyongyang, North Korea, as my father's bridge. He stood on it sometime in the late fall of 1950, during the Korean War. When my father was dispatched to Pyongyang to photograph the city, he walked up to the old Angel's pavilion, which gave him an angel's-eye view of the city. Angel's panorama O beautiful! The gate the river the bridge O marvelous! Angels are waving to us. My father couldn't help being overwhelmed by the beauty of the panorama of Pyongyang despite the fact that the whole city had been bombed to the ground. Craters are formed, and the impression of traveling on the moon is born. An aerial view reveals that the angels are, in fact, gooks in white pajamas, normal for the daytime.

Fatigued by endless assignments to war zones and by watching the plight of refugees, my father asked to be relocated. In 1983, we moved from Hong Kong to Frankfurt. My mother collapsed from grief. The grief of departing, once again. And I paced back and forth on Eiserner Steg above the Main River to see if I could hear the laments of the bridge of my childhood. Eiserner Steg had its share of tragedy from bombs, speeches, salutes, which is to say, it had its own particular angels who arrived, then departed. How did I happen to detect the laments of Glienicker Brücke? I owe it all to the ring of Benz. The ring spins, emitting exact hours of grief, deferred or not, through grandfather clocks, standard wall clocks, radios, and even swans. You could say that the ring is responsible for emitting signs of utilitarian purpose as well as occasional beauty. And Langenscheidt-brücke, which I think of as Damiel's bridge, turned out to be a mere twenty-minute walk from my apartment. One of the mysteries of memory is that sometimes home—particularly bridges—appears painfully remote. But the future juxtaposes.

= Damiel = Homer = Albert Camus = Frantz Fanon = W. E. B. Du Bois = Enola Gay = Little Boy = Tarzon bomb = the hollow world = the swan = my mother = my father = napalm = Mekong Delta = Miami = Gwangju = my sister = the departing angels = the identical sneakers = the eyes of a sparrow = my Berlin apartment = the ring of Benz = the boy = the funnel of light = the horizontal world = the heartache = the rising moon = the handless clock = the chiming clock = the hour of grief = mother's umbrella = in neocolony = in colony = the laments = "in the Imperial Panorama . . . it did not matter where you began the cycle" (Walter Benjamin) = "I can't find Potsdamer Platz" (Homer) = "these roads will take you into your own country" (Muriel Rukeyser) = "the world seems to be sinking into dusk" (Homer) = "the mask of neocolonialism" (Frantz Fanon) = "fuse a dead world straight" (Muriel Rukeyser) = "I won't give up until I find Potsdamer Platz" (Homer) =

At Homer's Potsdamer Platz, I look up at the mirror in the sky. A lowly translator in sneakers. Stupid, stupid girl, my sister wrote in her letters. A stupid sparrow. I spot a Korean reunification pavilion, only visible to crows and pigeons, across from Haus Huth where the Brothers Grimm lived and worked. The Angel's pavilion my father walked up to in Pyongyang on a hill. A mirror's-eye view of the future. "What is it about peace that its inspiration is not enduring? Why is its story so hard to tell?"—Homer flops down on a chair in no-man's-land, once divided. Pyongyang and Berlin, once bombed and dead.

Langenscheidtbrücke is above the rail tracks, legless, yet the angels still bathed in evening dew, singing and crying, perched on nearby trees as if they had been waiting for me. Sparrow, what took you so long? How was it that they could speak the rippling language of my childhood? How did they know to wave? That I would return? Spree O beautiful! The gate the library the TV tower O marvelous! The overwhelming beauty of Berlin's panorama. I owe it entirely to wings of utopia.

MAY 18 1980   서울 MARTIAL LAW
_____

MAY 19, 1980, ┌ 서울역 앞 데모
         ☆   ├ 남대문 광장 데모
               └ 버스, 경찰 차사 수전

         25
MAY ~~☆~~ 1980,   서울에서 광주로
                        (자동차)
                 JIM LAURIE 와 OGUSHI

MAY 26, 1980 ☆ KOREAN TROOPS
_____ MOVE IN CITY
         ☆   (장정 - 밤 12시 부터
                    (25일)

MAY 27 1980,   광주에서 — SEOUL

GWANGJU 26.5.1980

The last time I visited my father in Sydney, he quickly jotted down for me a time line of where he was before and during the Gwangju Massacre of May 1980. Martial law was declared in Seoul. On May 19, he filmed a student protest against the military power. He said the protests were spreading in the southern regions of Korea. My father received a phone call from Gwangju, from a Seoul-based freelancer. I can't stay here anymore, he told my father. I need to get back to my home base. Big impact! he cried out. We didn't know it at the time, but the military had already moved into the city and was working with the police, using brutal force. Many people were arrested and killed. The freelancer's surname was also Choi. After Choi returned to Seoul, he never called in or showed up at the office. He was hiding because he was so afraid of what he had witnessed. The Seoul situation was boiling over. We went out to City Hall Square and didn't see any action, but we saw a small group of protesters marching up from the South Gate. Suddenly they changed their direction and marched back toward the gate.

The small group of protesters quickly grew so big. Just from several hundred to a hundred thousand, marching down to Seoul Rail Station. Most were university students. Before they reached the station, they switched direction once again toward South Gate. In the meantime, the police had already blocked the road to City Hall. To avoid being caught between the students and police, I begged a middle-aged woman if I could enter her residence to film the protest. She looked directly into my eyes, then let me into her three-story building, which was more like a barrack. She pointed to a narrow stairway that led to the rooftop. Several Korean journalists were already taking photographs, and one was holding a silent camera. Beautiful. It wasn't the right word for the occasion, but it's what came to me at the time because the rooftop offered a perfect panorama of the city. Some years later, after we moved to Australia, I happened to watch a Korean TV drama that used the clip I had filmed of the protest from the rooftop. I remembered then that I made a copy of my tape in Hong Kong before it was sent to New York. I mailed the tape to a friend of mine who handed it over to the police, and the police later shared it with Korean TV stations. This is how your older brother was released from his military service after he suffered an injury and was let out of Korea during the most repressive dictatorship. It was a swap.

When we reached the outskirts of Gwangju, the military had blockaded the entire city. The soldier first denied our entry, but later he let us through because the driver convinced him that the American, the producer Jim Laurie, who was sitting in the front seat, was from the embassy. We passed through the cordon and drove around the city. Gwangju was in a state of total collapse. The city was dead. We drove down the main street that led us to a building near the provincial hall. We walked ten to twelve steps down into what looked like a gymnasium. There were about ten coffins lined up, covered in flags and bloodstained clothing. Some had small photos or ID cards on them. It was very quiet inside except for one woman, crying. I filmed this scene. We couldn't stay in there long because of the stench. It was the same stench I remembered from Vietnam, in 1967, right after your younger brother was born. That night I was in the fields with the US Marines. I couldn't sleep, so I moved to a different spot and laid my rain poncho on the ground to sleep. The same stench as Gwangju. Another time, I was on a Chinook copter, and two seats from me was a soldier's body. The same stench.

We were a three-member team—Jim Laurie the producer, Ogushi the Japanese sound-man, and myself. The driver also stayed with us at the beautiful traditional Korean inn. There was only one restaurant open in the city, just for the foreign press. Spicy stew, rice, and kimchi. The stew didn't look edible to me, yet nobody uttered a single complaint, not even Jim Laurie, who had teased and called me Mr. Kimchi only a few days before at Lotte Hotel in Seoul. I think the most violent acts against the civilians carried out by the military were already over by the time we reached Gwangju. As I said before, the freelancer who called me from Gwangju disappeared. That night I heard a noise—someone banging on the door. I mumbled to myself, son of a bitch. It must be police checking up on us. But I heard Mr. Hwang's voice, a journalist who had been with the Associated Press for thirty years. He was also staying at the inn. Then I heard the voice of a young boy. He could've been a shoeshine boy, perhaps a student. Mister, please you must get a move on. You can't sleep now. All the troops are moving in to occupy Gwangju. In fact, they're already here. Please be careful. If they see you moving about in the dark, they'll kill you. Stay alert and take care of yourselves. If I spend the night here, I'll get caught by the soldiers in the morning. I know my way around. Don't worry, I'm leaving the city. I just stopped by to warn you. Goodbye. My heart ached, and I remembered a scene from *Les Misérables*. Marius writes his farewell love letter to Cosette and hands it to a boy. The boy knows exactly where to find Cosette. He walks the streets of Paris, dark and dead like Gwangju.

I slept till 4:30 in the morning. We were the first group to go out. The driver was ready for us. We loaded our gear. About ten minutes after we got on the road, we heard shooting nearby. The driver hesitated, then drove on. There was a bus in front of the provincial hall. About twenty to thirty young men aged about twenty-two to twenty-seven were being arrested. They all looked pale, boarding the bus one by one. Some gave us a hint of a smile. Nobody said anything. Nobody tried to escape. Ogushi and I looked around the building. I think somebody called us. We looked up at the wide staircase. A major gestured silently, curling his index finger. He must have been educated in a US military school because no Korean would make that kind of finger gesture. I was worried that he would confiscate my videotapes, but he didn't even check my ID. He opened the door to a large hall to let us in, then closed the door behind us. It was pitch-dark inside. Black curtains over all the windows. Perhaps the hall was used for showing films. The major didn't speak to us at all. In retrospect, I think he thought we were a Japanese TV crew. We took a few steps forward and saw a body in a sitting position, leaning slightly forward. He had a good build and was at least 170 centimeters tall. He was burnt. I mean his skin was totally burnt. The strange thing was, why was his back bent 20 degrees forward? There was a sliver of light coming through the window where the curtain was not fully closed. I filmed this scene. The major gestured. Thumbs-up. Thumbs-down.

I gathered that the young man must have been one of the key leaders of the uprising. He had either burnt himself or he was killed. Either way, strangely enough, his body was leaning 20 degrees forward. I couldn't think too much about it then. I was more afraid of the major. After I filmed the scene, I opened the door and walked out with Ogushi. I feared that the major would detain us, but he let us leave. All the way to Seoul, I went back and forth in my head whether I should tell Jim Laurie about the scene I had filmed. If I had, in a matter of minutes the news about the young man would be transmitted via wire service to Tokyo, from Tokyo to New York, and from New York to all around the world. Then a few hours later, the Seoul police would track down his family and relatives. And they'd immediately be put under surveillance or arrested and lose their jobs. To this day, I don't regret not telling my producer. My tape was sent to New York, and maybe it's somewhere in a warehouse. There were rumors then that about 200 were buried somewhere in Gwangju. The dead young man would know. My guess is that there were a lot more than 200. I know at least one who didn't end up in the ground. The boy who stopped by to alert us of danger and said goodbye.

As my father scribbled the stars consciously or unconsciously, did he hear their silent lament? Or did they spontaneously appear to him? A star diving straight to earth, undoubtedly. A mysterious fingertip—possibly a zero—falling alongside the shooting star. The tail end of a comet above a star. I filmed this scene. The same stench of war. A fingertip or zero from the sky transfigures 200 into 2000. The boy who briefly stopped at the inn transposes Gwangju to Paris. The young man's crisp skin. Strangely 20 degrees forward. Zero lament. A sliver of light from the window. I filmed this scene. The major's language of American gestures. Index finger curls. Repeatedly. Thumbs-up. Thumbs-down. Repeatedly. A translator's language of angels. A zero in the sky. A dead city below. Beautiful. I translate it. Sky exchange.

I dreamt this morning that I was on a train passing across the Hangang rail bridge, or was it Eiserner Steg? In my dreams, disparate places are seamlessly linked. Anyhow, the train sped over the bridge so swiftly that it induced vertigo while I was still asleep. I let out the same cry whenever a swift flew into my Berlin apartment through the north-facing window. Ah, ah, ah.

I stood outside of Gwangju Provincial Hall where my father might have also stood thirty-six years earlier. At the 5.18 Archives, I was told by one of the researchers that the well-built body of the young man my father mentioned was very likely to have been that of Yun Sang-won, a leader of the civilian militia that resisted the massacre. The researcher showed me a copy of *Kwangju in the Eyes of the World*. I photographed it.

A sliver of a fingertip points to the outline of Korea. It might as well be the side view of a rabbit with a severed waist. A rabbit on the moon. The southwestern region where the city of Gwangju is located points back at the fingertip. A rabbit on the moon. They're irrationally linked. A sliver of grey on the left paves the way. The dark strips are the photos of Yun Sang-won, cropped. His body is lying flat on a checkered linoleum floor. A horizontal world. A zero degree. A rabbit on the moon.

Yes. Korea. Korean. My Hong Kong Adult ID was issued in August 1980, three months after the Gwangju democratic uprising. Until now, I'd remained unaware of the obvious link. The official seal and date of my existence. I translate it. I think of the lone ring of O outside my apartment window. A zero ring. A halo within a halo. Korea within a Korean. o o o roll down my hair. I have on a crown of zeros. Numbers blacked out are like the eyebrows drawn so far together in their grief that one might have supposed them blindfolded.

E7

SECRET

PAGE 01   SEOUL 05907 090944Z
ACTION NODS-00

INFO OCT-01 ADS-00 /001 W
                    ------------------035246 090945Z /11
O 090939Z MAY 80
FM AMEMBASSY SEOUL
TO SECSTATE WASHDC IMMEDIATE 6188

S E C R E T SEOUL 05907
                    DECAPTIONED

NODIS CHEROKEE

E.O. 12065:RDS-3 5/9/00 (GLEYSTEEN, W.H.) OR-M
TAGS: PGOV, PINT, PINS; KS, US
SUBJECT: KOREA FOCUS: MEETINGS WITH GENERAL CHUN AND
-          BLUE HOUSE SYG CHOI

1. (S) ENTIRE TEXT.

2. IT IS PHYSICALLY IMPOSSIBLE FOR ME TONIGHT TO RECORD
MY LONG CONVERSATIONS TODAY. I WILL DO SO TOMORROW. THE
SESSION WITH GENERAL CHUN DOO HWAN (M-R: CHON TU-HWAN)
WENT QUITE WELL. I GOT MY POINTS ACROSS WITHOUT SOURING
THE ATMOSPHERE OR ENGAGING IN ANY ARGUMENT WITH HIM.
MOREOVER, IN A VERY LONG DISCUSSION OF THE STUDENT SECURITY
SITUATION, I THINK HE PROBABLY FOUND MY ATTITUDE SYMPA-
THETIC. FROM WHAT CHUN TOLD ME, LATER CONFIRMED BY MY
CONVERSATION WITH KWANG SOO CHOI (M-R: CH'OE KWANG-SU),
I FEEL THE AUTHORITIES HAVE ADOPTED A SENSIBLE, PRUDENT
APPROACH TO THE STUDENT PROBLEM. THEY HAVE GIVEN IT A
GOOD DEAL OF THOUGHT AND THEY ARE VERY AWARE OF THE
DANGER OF OVER REACTION AND USE OF MILITARY FORCE.

3. MY SESSION WITH CHOI TURNED OUT TO BE A LONG EXPOSITION
OF HOW THE BLUE HOUSE SEES THE SITUATION AND PLANS TO
PROCEED. IN SHORT, THERE IS NO CHANGE IN THE POLITICAL
SCHEDULE, CAUTION REGARDING HANDLING OF THE STUDENT AND
   SECRET

   SECRET

PAGE 02   SEOUL 05907 090944Z

LABOR SITUATIONS, AND A GOOD DEAL OF MOROSENESS BROUGHT
ON BY THE STUDENT CHALLENGE AND THE UNHELPFUL POSTURE OF
THE POLITICAL OPPOSITION.

4. A BY-PRODUCT OF BOTH CONVERSATIONS IS THAT I HAVE
UNDERTAKEN TO CAUTION KIM YOUNG SAM (M-R: KIM YONG-SAM)
AND KIM DAE JUNG (M-R: KIM TAE-CHUNG) ABOUT THE RISKS THEY
ARE RUNNING OF THEY FAN THE FLAMES. I HAVE ALREADY ASKED
TO SEE BOTH OF THEM EARLY NEXT WEEK. GLEYSTEEN

SECRET

NNN

I notice **CHEROKEE**

공=o=5=O=zero

2 o, o, o, o, o, o, o, o, o, o, o, o, o, o, o, o, o, o, oo, o,

o, o, o, o, o, o, o, o, o, o, o, o, o, o, o, o, o, o, o, o, o,

o, oo, o, o, o, o, o, o, o, o, oo, o, o, o, o, o, o, o, o, o

roll down my hair

2 공공공공공공공공공공공공공공공공공공
공공공공공공공공공공공공공공공공공공
공공공공공공공공공공공공공공공공공공
공공

I notice ㄱ eyebrows

I notice ㅗ vowels

I notice ㅇ consonants

so far together in grief

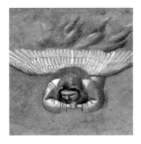

IN SHORT, THERE IS NO CHANGE IN THE neoliberal schedule

A GOOD DEAL OF consciousness

A BY-PRODUCT gasoline

FAN THE FLAMES swan

F 6t ?   67240

: ▆▆▆▆ SUMMARY: THIS REPORT TRANSMITS INFORMATION WHICH
(DATES THE SITUATION IN KWANGJU, KS.

8A. (U) DETAILS:

(1) ▆▆▆▆▆▆▆▆ AT 1830 HOURS 21 MAY LOCAL TIME, ▆▆▆▆▆ grief
REPORTED THAT THE KWANGJU SITUATION HAD WORSENED. ROK ARMY
OFFICERS IN THE SEOUL AREA HAD NOT BEEN TOLD THE "WHOLE
TRUTH" HOWEVER ▆▆▆▆ I HAD TALKED TO ▆▆▆▆ the angels, ▆▆▆▆
▆▆▆▆▆▆▆▆▆▆▆▆▆▆▆▆▆▆▆▆▆▆▆▆ WHO STATED THAT
CASUALTIES WERE VERY SERIOUS ON BOTH SIDES. ▆▆▆▆▆▆ STATED
THAT THE SITUATION HAD DETERIORATED DURING THE DAY AND THAT
NOT ALL INFORMATION WOULD BE PASSED TO US AUTHORITIES SINCE
MOST OF THE REPORTING WAS CAVEATED THE EQUIVALENT OF US
▆▆▆▆

(2) ▆blindfolded▆ WITHIN THIS CONTEXT, ▆▆▆▆▆▆▆ STATED THAT
RIOTING HAD SPREAD WITHIN CHOLLA NAM PROVINCE TO INCLUDE
NAJU AND SOME OTHER TOWNS. ▆▆▆ ESTIMATED CASUALTIES AS AT
LEAST 500 TOTAL ON BOTH SIDES, WITH DEATHS UNKNOWN.

(3) overwhelmed▆ RIOTERS IN KWANGJU HAD DESTROYED TAX
OFFICES, GOVERNMENT OFFICES AND WERE HOLDING HOSTAGES,
AMONG THEM SOME PROVINCIAL OFFICIALS. RIOTERS HAD ALSO
CAPTURED A HROF ARMORY TO INCLUDE RIFLES AND AMMUNITION;
MOST OF THE CASUALTIES WERE AMONG THIS CATEGORY, WHERE
TROOPS WERE AUTHORIZED TO SHOOT IF ABSOLUTELY NECESSARY OR
THEIR LIVES WERE IN DANGER. AT LEAST TWO APCS HAD ALSO
BEEN CAPTURED. ▆▆▆▆ I COMPARED SITUATION AT SOME LENGTH
TO TONG HAK REBELLION (CIRCA 1886).

(4) ▆▆▆▆▆▆▆ eyebrows were drawn AT 1600 HOURS 21 MAY THAT

PAGE 2   ▆▆▆ so far together ▆▆▆▆   00101110

DEPARTMENT OF DEFENSE
JOINT CHIEFS OF STAFF
MESSAGE CENTER

PAGE 3   67240

Their lament resounded in the very silence

endless calamities   AT THE TIME OF THIS REPORT, TELEPHONE
SERVICE TO THE KWANGJU AREA HAS BEEN TERMINATED, POSSIBLY
BY THE MILITARY AUTHORITIES. their grief IS OF THE HIGHEST
CALIBER AND CONFIRMED STRIPPING STORIES PREVIOUSLY REPORTED
eyebrows

(5)   REPORTED AT 1930 HOURS LOCAL
TIME 21 MAY THAT THREE INDEPENDENT SOURCES HAD REPORTED A
GROWING ANTI-AMERICAN FLAVOR TO RECENT EVENTS. Their lament
CHARACTERIZED THESE FEELINGS AS "EXTREMELY STRONG" AND
STATED THAT THE US DECISION TO RELEASE ROK OPCON FORCES
FOR RIOT CONTROL DUTY IN KWANGJU HAD GREATLY INCREASED
THIS ANTI-AMERICAN MOOD.

8B. (U) ORIG CMTS: NONE.

9. (U) PROJ NO: N/A
10.
11.
12.

13.
8T
#6480
ANNOTES
EW 117

PAGE 3   00101110

NNNN
220306Z

= I had talked to the angels, about the hours of grief. Little Boy dropped on Hiroshima at 08:15. General Chun's special forces deployed from the DMZ to Gwangju, a zone of massacre, at **18:30, 16:00, 19:30** ███████████ **REPORTED** ██████████ =

= Blindfolded within this context, your hands, in Vietnam, 1967. I was five. Mekong Delta. Operation Junction City. War Zone C =

= I had talked to the angels, about the gestures of grief. Their arms flung back with splayed hands =

= In the very silence, your hands are drawn so far together. Your fingers interlocked like feathers. Your pinkies meet to form a halo. You endure a hollow world =

= Two planets align in a straight line with your eye, irrationally. What hour, Father? =

= In the very silence, you hold up your arm, your fingers curl helplessly. Thumbs-up. A sensible sign. **GROWING ANTI-AMERICAN FLAVOR** =

= A zero stares out from the halved black moon. **THIS ANTI-AMERICAN MOOD** =

= Curiously enough, I **COMPARED SITUATION AT SOME LENGTH TO TONG HAK REBELLION (CIRCA 1886)**, a peasant revolt against Korea's ruling class =

= Thumbs-up = Thumbs-up = Thumbs-up =

At the 5.18 Archives, I noticed a photograph of a clock tower in the city of Gwangju taken during the citizens' armed insurgency against the brutal military forces, followed by a peaceful and mutual-aid self-governance. **ANTI-AMERICAN MOOD.** Its hour is 11:35 —likely, a few days after **THE US DECISION**, which had unleashed what Ken Saro-Wiwa calls "monstrous domestic colonialism," meaning, in the Gwangju context, tear gas, helicopters, tanks, bullets, batons, and bayonets. Likely the same bayonets used in Vietnam, meaning the same South Korean soldiers who committed massacres against the Vietnamese civilians. The US-ROK decision. Thoroughly neocolonial.

Georgy Katsiaficas compares the Gwangju uprising "to that of the Paris Commune in French history, and of the battleship *Potemkin* in Russian history." **"EXTREMELY STRONG"** As Frantz Fanon has observed, "there exists a sort of detached complicity between capitalism and the violent forces which blaze up in colonial territory" "we are dealing with a strategy of immediacy . . . the aim and the program of each locally consti-tuted group is local liberation. If the nation is everywhere, then she is here." The cur-rent official death toll is 165, but poet Kim Hyesoon tells me that nobody believes it. The military destroyed its records and discarded the corpses into the sea and earth. **WITH DEATHS UNKNOWN**, 0=5=0 forever stamped onto our collective memory.

DENKT AN KWANG JU. In the future city of two Koreas, a full moon rises above **KOREA. SÜD** is no longer relevant. Just think. ROK is OK, and therefore, obsolete. In the future, the US thinks of Gwangju, Hiroshima, Mekong Delta, even Chinook and Cherokee. And Miami—a war zone, erupting from within. In the future, my father's fingers curl in reverie. The boy returns to the inn to bid farewell as the clock chimes. A deferred heartache.

Denkt an. And I think of the clock on the wall behind Yi Sang in shirt and tie with suspenders. His scruffy hair stands tall above his youthful hairline. During the height of Japanese colonial oppression, he posed with his writer friends at a publishing house where he worked before departing to Tokyo in 1936. The following year, Yi Sang was arrested and died from tuberculosis at the hospital of Tokyo Imperial University.

Denkt an. Forty-four years later, an old-fashioned clock on the wall of the meeting room at Provincial Hall in Gwangju. Maybe it's the twin clock of Yi Sang's or Imamura's. A German photojournalist Jürgen Hinzpeter filmed it. It's almost noon. Negotiations with the military are being conducted over the phone by the representatives of Gwangju citizens.

Denkt an. Walter Benjamin—"the realm of the mark is a medium" "the mark appears principally on living beings (Christ's stigmata, blushes, perhaps leprosy and birthmarks)" "the mark is always absolute and resembles nothing else in its manifestation" "because it appears on living beings, the mark is so often linked to guilt (blushing) or innocence (Christ's stigmata)" "*temporal* magic appears in the mark in the sense that the resistance of the present between the past and the future is eliminated" "magically fused."

Yi Sang's clock chimes, leaving a trail of cosmic dust and stars. The distant, traveling medium of the mark across time and space can also be said to be an absolute mark. Magically fused time is never exact or predictable. It only knows how to manifest itself through its twins. Temporal magic frequently manifests as numbers, as zeros. They're like the pockmarks left on a face or FOIA page. They're entirely unavoidable.

Grief has a tendency to migrate from clock to clock, war to war, massacre to massacre, colony to neocolony. I notice grief has a lone wing, an absolute mark, resembling nothing else. What else can grief see? Saturn perhaps. Nine years later, a hand appears to adjust the clock, the hour of Little Boy.

Denkt an. Absolute grief. Absolute sign. Fingertip, leaf, or wing. However, gestures such as thumbs-up, thumbs-down, or curling of the index finger are out of the equation. These are mere military signs, historically. What's deferred is often defused, dissipated, faintly disclosed. Such is the nature of grief fused by temporal magic.

What else can grief see?

ABC News *World News Tonight*, New York, 27.5.1980

광주

The birthmark on my left thigh has faded over time. Maybe because I no longer wear boyish shorts as I used to when I was little. I rarely think about it now, yet as a child, I was frequently preoccupied with it. In Korean, a birthmark is commonly referred to as a "pig's freckle." I detested it and blushed whenever my mother pointed at my mark and uttered "돼지점." I could never make out the shape of my absolute mark. It certainly didn't look anything like a pig. It didn't resemble the map of Korea either. The mark, to me, is as nebulous as a cloud. Hence, my guilt is also nebulous—likely deferred. I conclude that there's no temporal magic to a stupid, stupid girl, a stupid sparrow with a pig's freckle.

점

27.3.1967 [I was five—the pinnacle of my pig's freckle]

NBC when. REPORTER

without (alone in hardship)

MEKONG DELTA region's

enemy search & destroy OPERATION

HITTLEBURG at AP

journalist photographed [me]

7.7.1972
alone in hardship yet you stupid stupid girl
with a pig's freckle jolly-polly on a plane
like a humpty-점pty-sat-on-a-wall
so fickle with her freckle
kill kill kill
yet [me] photographed you

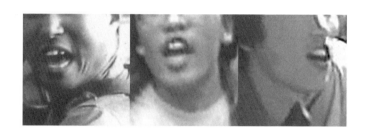

공=0=5=O=zero

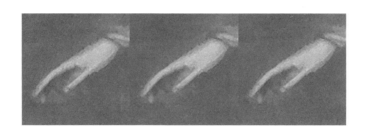

DENKT AN GWANGJU

DENKT AN MIAMI

! ! !

20일 「리버티」지구에서 소방관들이 鎭火작업을 벌이는 가운데 州방위軍이 경비하고 있다. 【AP연합】

MIAMI 18.5.1980

The news of the Gwangju massacre and rebellion was covered up by the military government during and after, for seven years, by arresting and torturing thousands. Hence, it was only sensible that on May 23, 1980, *Seoul Shinmun* reported on the "Miami riot" instead, which took place during the same days as the "Gwangju riot." Empire is everywhere.

In Miami, a strategy of immediacy against the injustice erupted when four policemen were acquitted of beating insurance salesman and former marine Arthur McDuffie to death, with their flashlights, after he was already handcuffed. *The Washington Post* reports on May 19, 1980: "Billowing clouds of smoke and bright flames spread across the night sky as gunfire, beatings and arson continued through a second night of a massive race riot here." Likewise, **RIOTERS IN KWANGJU HAD DESTROYED** TV stations, tax offices, government offices.

I compare the situation at some length to Fanon's theory on violence—"illuminated by violence, the consciousness of the people rebels against any pacification" "we should flatly refuse the situation to which the Western countries wish to condemn us" "for centuries the capitalists have behaved in the underdeveloped world like nothing more than war criminals" "deportations, massacres, forced labor, and slavery have been the main methods" "the political militant is the rebel" "to fight the war and to take part in politics" "the two things become one and the same."

The boy returns. This time to the rubble of a war zone within. He rides his bicycle through the streets of Miami, dark and dead like Gwangju. Empire is everywhere. I'll be frank: police brutality, one of "the main methods" against Black people, is war. Judith Butler—"we might think of war as" "dividing populations into those" "who are grievable and those who are not" "an ungrievable life is one that cannot be mourned because it has never lived" "that is" "it has never counted as a life at all." The boy lives. In the future, every hour is grievable.

From Potsdamer Platz to Kreuzberg, I came upon W. E. B. Du Bois. I noticed a small leaf like a butterfly wing on the top right corner of the plaque. An absolute mark, signaling to me. I also spotted Walter Benjamin not far from the park near my apartment. Benjamin was born the same year Du Bois came to Berlin to work on his dissertation. They are now fused in my mind. Another case of temporal magic, in my opinion. Du Bois—"it is a peculiar sensation" "this double-consciousness" "this sense of always looking at one's self through the eyes of others" "one ever feels his twoness" "two souls" "two thoughts" "two unreconciled strivings" "two warring ideals in one dark body" "shut out from their world by a vast veil."

The vast veil, when stretched across the Pacific Ocean, has a different function. Its militarization is ever heightened to contain the imagined enemy, to perpetuate imperial hegemonic control. The so-called Manifest Destiny is woven into its every fiber. The veil manifests as an endless barbed wire fence across the DMZ of two Koreas. The veil of unreasonableness. My twoness is born out of national division. My other is perpetually Red, ready to nuke or be nuked. My twinness manifests within unreasonable destiny, vast homesickness. My twin self has my comb. She remembers my flowered shirt and shorts, a hairpin in my hair. She remembers me as a child. She instructs me to return. She forgets that sparrows can't return.

When I went back to Benjamin's plaque with Sasha Dugdale, who was visiting me from West Sussex, she pointed out how the word *suicide* in German was *Freitod*—free death. At that moment, a panorama of free death appeared before my eyes.

NEWSWEEK 2.6.1986—"Down with Chun Doo Hwan!" "Down with dictatorship!" "thousands of angry students" "commemorating the nearly 200 people killed by Army troops" "in the southern city of Kwangju" "Lee Dong Soo, 22, screamed, 'Out with U.S. imperialists'" "doused himself with gasoline" "then he set himself afire" "and toppled in flames to his death." I notice his splayed hands. One lit like a torch. Straight arms slide down a wall or war. Helpless legs fracture rays of light or hours. Eternal clouds = Spontaneous combustion = Uncombed hair. A triad of perpendicularity ㄱ = ⊥ = ○. Evidently all angels are spheres, uttered motherless tongues. I pity the ones without shoes or boots. When the Korean War broke out, my father couldn't leave Seoul—even when his mentor Paek Un-seon asked my father to go with him—because he'd left his beloved camera at the office, at the *Dong-a Daily*. In a hurry, he only managed to grab a small sticky patch of cyanide from the darkroom. He kept it in his pocket in case he was captured and forced to fight in the war. To choose free death over brutal death. My sister, one day, in Australia, ordered a box of cyanide from a lab. She was a scientist, hence normal for the daytime. Like an angel or butterfly wing, she swiftly entered her bedroom with a glass of water and spoon and locked the door. My father pleaded with her. Free death over brutal death. Brutal death over free death. To choose neither under empire. Two thoughts, uttered motherless tongues. Evidently zeros fall down my hair, normal for the daytime. Stupid, stupid girl, sparrows chirp to me in Berlin.

DFF *Aktuelle Kamera*, East Germany, 22.5.1980

KWANGDSCHU

—Benjamin's Telephone—

—And the voice that slumbered in those instruments was a newborn voice—

(((((할로)))))

—Each day and every hour, the telephone was my twin brother—

It's true that angels keep a tally of blazing eyebrows on earth

—To the despondent who wanted to leave this wicked world, it shone with the light of
a last hope—

**Regardless of the chorus, incessant motherless tongues, my head dives as an
icy comet**
O flurry of hair or hope

—I tore off the two receivers, which were heavy as dumbbells, thrust my head between
them, and was inexorably delivered over to the voice that now sounded—

**For some time now, perhaps eternally, smoke has billowed out my ears, as I
sing, Freitod, Freitod**
Splayed hands, mine and not mine, flicker like sparrow wings

—There was nothing to allay the violence with which it pierced me—

Sensibly, I swoon like a newborn and remember
that all angels are spheres, they manifest as snow

—Powerless, I suffered, seeing that it obliterated my consciousness of time—

Hallo-hallo, I sing to the universe as my feet and ankles dissolve across the
sky
O flimsy dresses

—And just as the medium obeys the voice that takes possession of him from beyond
the grave, I submitted to the first proposal that came my way through the telephone—

Free death, free death, hello!

o o   o o

o   o   oo oo   o

o   o   o

oo

freitod, freitod

—tod-tod-tod-tod-tod—

a nightingale sang *Fade far away, dissolve, and quite forget*

and thought

two thoughts

ffree, ffree

trills of consonants

공공

fall down my hair

—stupi-stupi—

sparrows chirp to me

because

73

because Septimus had said, I will kill myself;
an awful thing to say

; ; ; ; ;

pick-up-the-phone!

—ck-ck-ck-ck-ck—

sparrows again

hallo, hallo

a ring of zeros

(((((공)))))

So, thought Septimus,
looking up, they are signalling to me

—점-p-점-p-점-p—

sparrowstod

Septimus, Septimus,
they sang in voices

Adieu! Adieu! sang nightingale

adieu and awful not remembering but the phone rang regardless

"Mr. Choi is missing in action

somewhere in Cambodia or Laos"

expectedly, Mrs. Choi fell gravely ill

while filming wars

he often detected the frequency of perpendicularity

돈나, 돈미

ㄴ, ㄴ

a world of eyebrows

upside down

he said my sister and I often flashed before his eyes

we were a panorama of sparrows under Mother's umbrella

—ffrei-ffrei-ffrei-ffrei-ffrei-ffrei—

sparrows sang to me

ffree-girls-with-halobands

hallo, hallo

할로

ㅎ ㅎ   ㅎ ㅎ

ㅎ   ㅎ   ㅎㅎ   ㅎㅎ   ㅎ

ㅎ   ㅎ   ㅎ

ㅎingularity of snow

ist lone eye-brow-lash

fall adieu-adieuciously at night

we chirp and chirp

after Septimus

this beauty, this exquisite beauty

ㄹ

ㄹ

ㄹ

of billowing skirts

languishing and melting in the sky

o	a pan rama f ut pia	o
o	sparr w sparr w	o
o	sn w sn w	o
o	hell hell	o
o	c mb c mb	o
o	La s La s	o
o	what h ur, Father?	o
o	Camb dia Camb dia	o

zeros fall down my hair

and I'm still in ugly shorts

my sister's halo touches mine

엄-bre-lla-lla-bre-lla-lla

she calls and calls me

we are all angels, she said on the phone

and I submitted to her

Mother's umbrella,

a snowdrop

at that moment a panorama of motherless tongues appeared before my eyes

=ARE YOU ALIVE?=I AM ALIVE=

=ARE YOU FREE?=I AM FREE=

=ARE YOU 4.19.1960?=I AM 5.18.1980=

=ARE YOU SEOUL?=I AM MASAN=

=ARE YOU JEJU?=I AM YEOSU=

=ARE YOU GWANGJU?=I AM KWANGDSCHU=

=ARE YOU ALIVE?=I AM ALIVE=

=ARE YOU FREE?=I AM FREE=

The sparrows fluttering, rising, and falling

Once upon a time, a lone sparrow lived on Bruegel's or Tarkovsky's snowy crest. There also lived an orphan boy. The boy's hat, like my father's, had earflaps. His parents had perished during the siege of Leningrad or Kwangdschu. One day, unknowingly, the boy's heart ached. He took out a dummy grenade from his bag, which he had been carrying all his orphanhood. That day, a shooting practice went haywire. A bald spot on the drill ser-geant's scalp pulsated like a sparrow's heart. His memory of the crossing of Lake Sivash in 1943 appeared out of nowhere. It was winter after all. Memory blew in closer and closer like a balloon. As the orphan boy reached the snowy crest, whistling, his frozen tears dan-gled from his freckled cheeks. Why all the tears? Sparrow flew up and perched on his hat. Because of this beauty, this exquisite beauty of our sphere, our halo world.

/

the boy's about-turn of a century

/

= the liberation of Prague in 1945 =

= victory fireworks =

= Hitler's corpse = victory fireworks =

= a civilian with a crutch in despair =

= atom bomb mushroom cloud =

= LITTLE BOY of Hiroshima =

/

the boy's about-turn of a century

/

= Little Red Book =

= many faces of Mao =

= momentous parades of Mao =

= Sino-Soviet border dispute of 1969 =

/

sparrow's about-turn of a century

/

= April 1960 Student Revolution =

= many faces of general =

= Gwangju Uprising of 1980 =

= motherless tongues =

= wings of utopia =

/

There's no death on earth
There's just reality and light

(Arseny Tarkovsky)

just

eternal

boy

sparrow

snowdrop

all

perpendicular

under

Mother's umbrella,

a

mere

panorama

IMPERIAL PANORAMA 1980

"Imperial Panorama" and *"Critique of Violence,"* Walter Benjamin

AKTUELLE KAMERA, German Democratic Republic, 22.5.1980

Indictment to the World: White Paper on Atrocious Kwangju Genocide, issued by the Central Committee of the Revolutionary Party for Reunification, Pyongyang, Korea, 10.6.1980

부산일보, *Busan Ilbo*, 19.5.1980

"Miami Riot Continues," *Washington Post*, 19.5.1980

= *One of the great attractions of the travel scenes found in the Imperial Panorama was that it did not matter where you began the cycle* = AM VORABEND DES JUGENDFESTIVALS IN KARL-MARX-STADT On the eve of the youth festival in Karl-Marx-Stadt = DIE SOMMERSPIELE IN MOSKAU The summer games in Moscow = DER WARSCHAUER VERTRAG The Warsaw Treaty = SANKTIONEN GEGEN IRAN Sanctions against Iran = DIE US-KRIEGSMARINE IM PERSISCHEN GOLF The US Marines in the Persian Gulf = DÄNISCHE SPORTLER Danish athletes = AUCH LUXEMBURG Also Luxembourg = *But there was a small, genuinely disturbing effect that seemed to me superior* = **The Chon Du Hwan gang conducted an operation to mop up Kwangju** = *Militarism is the compulsory, universal use of violence as a means to the ends of the state* =

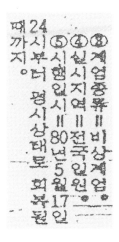

(3) Martial Law Type – Emergency Martial Law

(4) Region = Entire nation

(5) Effective date = From May 17 midnight until things return to normal

= DER AUFSTAND The uprising = *This was the ringing of a little bell that sounded a few seconds before each picture moved off with a jolt* = **the commander of the South Korea–US Combined Forces John Wickham to the Chon Du Hwan clique for suppression of the people's uprising in Kwangju** = *If that first function of violence is called the lawmaking function, this second will be called the law-preserving function = in order to make way first for an empty space and then for the next image* = DAS KRIEGSRECHTS The martial law = *Lawmaking is powermaking, assumption of power, and to that extent an immediate manifestation of violence* = **The whole city of Kwangju is a sea of blood** = DIE ARMEE The army = *And every time it rang, the mountains with their humble foothills, the cities with their mirror-bright windows* = **frantically brandished bayonets** = *the railroad stations with their clouds of dirty yellow smoke* = **Now Kwangju is completely blockaded from outside** = *the vineyards down to the smallest leaf* = DIE AUFSTÄNDISCHEN IN KWANGDSCHU The insurgents in Gwangju = **"Youngsters are all mobs. Kill them all"** = *Mythic violence is bloody power over mere life for its own sake = were suffused with the ache of departure* =

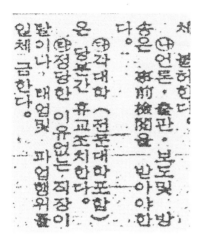

(b) media, publications, reports must receive inspection

(c) all universities (including vocational colleges) will shut down for the time being

(d) quitting work without any legitimate reason, work slowdown and strikes are banned

= *I formed the conviction that it was impossible to exhaust the splendors of the scene at just one sitting* = DAS WETTER The weather = *At its inception, they found their last audience in children* = OST UND WEST = SÜD UND NORD = *divine violence is pure power over all life for the sake of the living* =

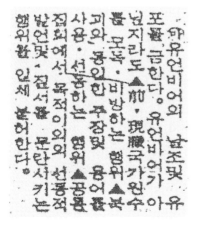

(e) fabrication and circulation of false rumors are banned even if they are not false rumors

▲ the act of defaming former and current heads of state ▲ the act of agreeing with and inciting the views and language of the North Korean puppet regime ▲ the act of making inflammatory statements at a public rally is not permitted

= *Distant worlds were not always strange to these arts* = TERROR GEGEN AFRO-AMERIKANER IN MIAMI Terror against African Americans in Miami = **Billowing clouds of smoke and bright flames spread across the night sky** = ALLER WELT All of the world = *God opposes myth, mythic violence is confronted by the divine* = *And it so happened that the longing such worlds aroused spoke more to the home than to anything unknown* = DIE MENSCHENRECHTE Human rights = *Justice is the principle of all divine endmaking* = **The acquittal Saturday in Tampa of the four ex-policemen in a televised trial inflamed Miami's black community, which has been protesting police brutality here for several years** = AFGHANISTAN = **Downtown Miami was eerie and deserted today** = DIE ANNEKTIONSMASSNAHMEN ISRAELS Israel's annexation measures = **Gas stations were closed** = **Black youths sped down the wide boulevards, shouting racial epithets and raising their fists in the sign of black power** = *if the former [mythic violence] is bloody, the latter [divine violence] is lethal without spilling blood* = DÜRREKATASTROPHE IN ÄTHIOPIEN Drought disaster in Ethiopia = **Block after block of gutted buildings burned quietly** = **Shouting a one-word battle cry—"McDuffie"** = *If mythic violence is lawmaking, divine violence is law-destroying* = **"I don't believe our police department is a brutal police department per se"** =

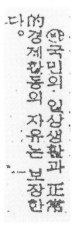

(f) the citizens' everyday life and the freedom of normal economic activities are ensured

= *[Police] power is formless, like its nowhere-tangible, all-pervasive, ghostly presence in the life of civilized states* = "We're professional. You do have isolated incidents like any other place" = SÜDKOREA—MEINE DAMEN UND HERREN South Korea—Ladies and Gentlemen = **Kwangju, a city of suffering, splashed with torrential blood and piled high with corpses, is indicting the human butchers to the whole world** = "But we also realize that if someone does something to us, they've got to be punished too" = *if mythic violence brings at once guilt and retribution, divine power only expiates* = UNTER PAK TSCHONG HI Under Park Chung Hee = **"No. 2 Pak Jong Hi gang"** = "Right now, it's a one-sided situation" = "I think this has been smoldering for a long time" =

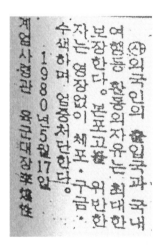

(g) the freedom of foreigners to enter the country and travel will be ensured

Anyone who violates this martial law proclamation will be arrested without a warrant

- detained
- interrogated
- dealt with severely

May 17, 1980, Commander in Chief of Martial Law, Army General, Yi Hui-seong

= MORGEN WOLKIG Tomorrow cloudy = *When it rained, there was no pausing out front to survey the list of fifty pictures* = BERLIN = *I went inside and found in fjords and under coconut palms the same light that illuminated my desk in the evening when I did my schoolwork* = CHILE = *It may have been a defect in the lighting system that suddenly caused the landscape to lose its color* = NIKARAGUA = *But there it lay, quite silent under its ashen sky* = GLÜCKLICHEN ZUKUNFT DER MENSCHHEIT Happy future of mankind = "SÄUBERUNGSAKTION" Cleanup operation = EL SALVADOR = DIE SANDINISTA = DIE USA-HEGEMONIE = 75-MILLIONEN-DOLLAR = *It was as though I could have heard even wind and church bells if only I had been more attentive* =

백부장은 마라톤선수 손기정。어
BERLIN 에서 (올림픽) 1등을 했을때
WIRE PHOTO가 들어왔을 가을의
멀보기를 지워 신문에 보도되어
신문에 폐간되고, 본인은 진역.
유명한 본었데, 6.25전쟁때
불행이도 이북에 납치되어 사망.
그분에 없는 신문사 생활에 싫어서
나와 그후 다시는 돌아가지 않음.

A panorama of divided identity. Sohn Kee-chung and Sohn Kee-chung. My father and the flag eraser Paek Un-seon of *Dong-A Ilbo*. A panorama of eyebrows.

"When Director Paek received the wired photo of the Korean marathon runner Sohn Kee-chung, who came in first in the Berlin Olympics of 1936, he scratched out the Japanese flag and published it. The newspaper was shut down, and Paek was imprisoned. He became famous, but unfortunately, during the Korean War he was kidnapped and taken to North Korea and perished. I didn't want to work without him, so I didn't go back."

The mark of the empire's flag appears principally on the marathon runner's chest. Because the mark appears on living beings, principally runners, blushing or not. Not a pig's freckle. Paek scratched it out because this particular mark is always absolute and resembles nothing else in its manifestation. Yet the hole in the runner's heart. In Berlin. Run. Mirror nation!

Nation is a nation is a nation is a nation

Nation is a nation is a nation is a nation

Nation is a nation is a nation is a nation

Nation is a nation is a nation is a nation

Nation is a nation is a nation is a nation

Swan is a swan is a swan is a swan

is a swan is

a swan

is a

s

FRANKFURT 1984

first—the mountains blushed before the closed eyelids—twinkling river enters—eyelids open like a crab's casement—only to see the mountains cooled like a blue cloud—snow snow snow—like a luminous object—when skinned—dissipates—any fracture on a veined leaf—wind is sent to a flooded beach—sights of momentary heights—like falling into an empty well—the effort to maintain a humid point could not match the taste of petals flavored by pollen grains—wee wee bee lands on twig's lips—meow—said the moon—fat snow had too much mud—angels bathing in mountain tea—lily wings—their dresses—ruby mist—singing—mirror narration—irregular waves—at times wives— travel to the world below—stirring echoes of the cars above—milky tiles reduce friction when angels flee their homes—a transparent tide rises to my thighs—spiky pebbles when drowned are most telling—to my feet—a gold peach never itches—blooming fingers—plum eyes—river inflamed by night—I have a thought jeweled by a jade—as large as a crater lake—swan swan swan

NOTES

"POTSDAM 11.2.1986": When I arrived in Berlin for my 2019 DAAD Artists-in-Berlin residency, my father told me that he had been in Berlin, winter of 1986. Then I happened to spot my father on Glienicker Brücke via YouTube. As when I spotted my father in the photo of the 1961 martial law declaration at the old Seoul City Hall (see *DMZ Colony*), I knew immediately that finding my father on the bridge between Berlin and Potsdam was the unfolding of *Mirror Nation*. Rbb media GmbH kindly granted me permission to use the three stills of my father.

The photos of the clocks are stills from *Black Rain* (1989) by Shōhei Imamura. This film has always haunted me. At first, I thought it was the hair falling out from radiation sickness. But when I watched again, it was also the clocks. As a photographer and cameraman, my father was preoccupied with time. In Vietnam, he squatted when he filmed, to be at eye level with the soldiers—the ground level of war. He counted the seconds before ducking down, and this may have saved his life many times over. I sent a letter to Imamura's son, Hirosuke Imamura of Imamura Productions. He then wrote back via email, and so I was able to send him an excerpt of the pieces with the clock images. I also translated them with Google Translate. He replied on July 29, 2021, and not surprisingly: "I don't fully understand it. But I somehow understood that you are not the owner of the opinion that justifies the atomic bombing, so I will grant you a posting." My guess is that he also used an online translator of sorts. The recurring images of clocks and the watches my father wore during his assignments in Vietnam are, for me, signs of grief—grief in time, hence, its eternal return. The time of crimes against humanity returning again and again as in *Black Rain*, and my father returning to me again and again in photographs. Every time I return to my father in Australia, he gifts me a wristwatch.

"BRIDGES OF =": Taedong Bridge photo is the one from *Hardly War*, my father's, taken in Pyongyang,

North Korea, sometime in October or November 1950, before the bridge was damaged. Hangang Bridge photo is by Jay Weaver. The Swan photo is by my father, In-Jip Choi. The Eiserner Steg photo by Walter Olshausen from Wikipedia Commons: *Eiserner Steg in Frankfurt gesprengt (Winter 1945/46)*. Excerpt from *Vertigo* by W. G. Sebald, translated by Michael Hulse: copyright © 1990 by Vito von Eichborn GmbH & Co Verlag KG, English translation copyright © 1999 by Michael Hulse. Reprinted by permission of New Directions Publishing Corp.

"Fatigued by endless assignments . . .": Langenscheidtbrücke is a bridge that appears in *Wings of Desire* (1987) by Wim Wenders. Damiel is one of the angels in the film.

"= Damiel = Homer = Albert Camus . . .": In *Wings of Desire*, "The Invocation of the World" takes place on Langenscheidtbrücke. Homer is an old man in the film, appearing at the Staatsbibliothek zu Berlin, Haus Potsdamer Straße and Potsdamer Platz. In my mind, Homer is my father's double, for he has also read and walked through the desolation of division and war—multiple wars, in fact. Quotes are from Walter Benjamin's "Imperial Panorama," Muriel Rukeyser's *The Book of the Dead*, and Frantz Fanon's *The Wretched of the Earth*.

"I dreamt this morning . . .": Whenever I return to Seoul, I walk on the Hangang Bridge, next to the place where I grew up. But somehow, I can never make myself cross all the way to the other side of the bridge. It feels as if I would never be able to come back if I did.

"I stood outside of Gwangju Provincial Hall . . .": Photo by Jay Weaver. The book I mention: *Kwangju in the Eyes of the World: The Personal Recollections of the Foreign Correspondents Covering the Kwangju Uprising* by Journalists Association of Korea edited by Amalie M. Weber (Pulbit Publishing, 1997).

"A sliver of a fingertip . . .": The photos of Yun Sang-won's body in *Kwangju in the Eyes of the World* are by an American journalist, Norman Thorpe.

"UNCLASSIFIED RELEASED IN FULL" and "DEPARTMENT OF DEFENSE": These two declassified documents were obtained with permission from the investigative journalist Tim Shorrock's website, which contains vital and extensive archives of Freedom of Information Act documents related to US policy in South Korea (see www.timshorrock.com/2022/09/01/key-foia-documents-on-gwangju-5-18/). The FOIA documents reveal the role the US played in the brutal suppression of the Gwangju Uprising 1980. The Gwangju Uprising is a key event marking the "overlapping histories" (to borrow Edward Said's term) of KORUS. And yet my chorus of O: the two FOIA documents are partly "collaged" with tracing paper, with Os traced over. Redacted spaces filled with photos of my father's hands, watches, and phrases from *Vertigo*.

"궁=0=5=O=zero": (See *Hardly War*.) (*DMZ Colony* has another kind of O: e=0|=10.) The photo of the angel is from Giotto di Bondone's *Lamentation* (The Mourning of Christ). I first encountered the lamenting angels in *Vertigo*. Somehow, I couldn't recover from the sight of their eyebrows, so I decided to visit the Arena Chapel in Padua in December 2019 and hear the angels in person. I adopted Sebald's recurring arrangement of photos in threes as a syntax for the language of grief, as it might have been for Sebald, too. = is also a syntax, a syntax that enables multiple places and times to coexist simultaneously. I inherited = from Aimé Césaire and Gertrude Stein. = has a double function. It also functions as an anti-neocolonial sign, which is to say translation is an anti-neocolonial mode (see *DMZ Colony*).

"SÜD KOREA DENKT AN KWANG JU": A poster made by Koreans in West Germany in 1980 to raise awareness and protest the massacre. This poster was on display at 5.18 Archives when I visited Gwangju in 2016 and also in 2022.

"At the 5.18 Archives …": Ken Saro-Wiwa's quote is from *Genocide in Nigeria: The Ogoni Tragedy* (Saros International Publishers, 1992).

"Georgy Katsiaficas compares …": Quotes are from "Remembering the Gwangju Uprising" by Georgy Katsiaficas in *South Korean Democracy: Legacy of the Gwangju Uprising* (Routledge, 2006), edited by Georgy Katsiaficas and Na Kahn-chae. And *The Wretched of the Earth* by Frantz Fanon, translated by Constance Farrington (Grove Press, 1963). The official death toll mentioned is from "2 Days in May That Shattered Korean Democracy" by Tim Shorrock and Injeong Kim, May 28, 2020, *The Nation*.

"Denkt an. And I think of the clock …": Photo of Yi Sang and colleagues are in the public domain.

"Denkt an. Forty-four years later …": German ARD reporter Jürgen Hinzpeter filmed the uprising in

Gwangju. While in Berlin, I obtained a viewing copy of *Südkorea am Scheideweg* (South Korea at a Crossroads), a documentary film Hinzpeter produced for NDR in 1980. I watched it several times, listening intently to the German. Later, my German-language teacher Susanne Fladt-Bruno kindly offered to transcribe the narration for me, which then enabled me to use DeepL Translate. This is the documentary that was secretly taken into South Korea in the early 1980s and was circulated at universities and in grassroots organizations underground. Hinzpeter's insightful documentary played a key role in raising awareness of the Gwangju Uprising of May 1980. When I finally noticed the "old-fashioned clock," I knew instantly that the clock was what needed translating.

"Denkt an. Walter Benjamin . . .": From "Painting, or Signs and Marks," translated by Rodney Livingstone, in Walter Benjamin, *Selected Writings: 1913–1926*, vol. 1, edited by Marcus Bullock and Michael W. Jennings (The Belknap Press of Harvard University Press, 1996).

"What else can grief see?": Photo of me by my father on July 7, 1972, on our flight from Seoul to Hong Kong.

The stills are from my father's film, broadcast on ABC News *World News Tonight*, May 27, 1980. My father also filmed the students singing, protesting, and running in downtown Seoul on May 19, 1980. Courtesy of ABC News. To see what grief sees. I see clocks of the world, every minute hand when bombs dropped over the heads and houses. My father running. Thumbs-up, thumbs-down. Homer sitting in an armchair at Potsdamer Platz. A stupid girl in the mirror. Now what? Grief tells me to live.

"ABC News *World News Tonight* . . .": Courtesy of ABC News. I was given permission to use this image with only the partial map of Korea.

"Chorus of O": Close-ups: my father running in Mekong Delta; college students running and protesting in Seoul; and middle- and high-school students protesting in Gwangju.

"DENKT AN GWANGJU / DENKT AN MIAMI": The hand (repeated three times) is from Giotto di Bondone's *Joachim's Sacrifice*. Photo taken at the Arena Chapel.

"MIAMI 18.5.1980": When I visited *Seoul Shinmun* in September 2022, the archivist gave me permission to use the partial image of the newspaper in print. The Miami photo by Kathy Willens courtesy of AP. The photo of the boy on a bicycle is *McDuffie Riots 1980* by Bill Frakes, from the *Miami Herald* © 1980, McClatchy. All rights reserved. Used under license.

Fanon quotes are from *The Wretched of the Earth*. Judith Butler quotes are from *Frames of War: When Is Life Grievable?* (Verso, 2009).

"BERLIN 30.11.2019": W. E. B. Du Bois quotes are from *The Souls of Black Folk* (Pocket Books, 2005). I read Du Bois because Robert Hass mentioned "double-consciousness" to me after I read from "A Journey from Neocolony to Colony" at Community of Writers in June 2014. Silvia Fehrmann, the current director of the DAAD Artists-in-Berlin program, told me that, while she was serving on the historical committee, she fought for Du Bois's plaque—it was a way of conceding to the memorial plaque for David Bowie. I walked past Du Bois's plaque many times on my way to daad-galerie in preparation for my exhibition *DMZ Colony: Exhibition of a Book* (March 2020).

"NEWSWEEK 2.6.1986": The left image is from *Grandes Heures de Rohan* (1401–1500), in the public domain, Bibliothèque nationale de France. Jennifer Scappettone used it as a background image for an online Exploratory Translation Colloquium, which I participated in with Jen Hofer on February 16, 2021. Jennifer gave a short but brilliant introduction about the image of the falling figure from the Tower of Babel. When I returned to the recording of the event, so I could listen to the introduction again, I found out that this portion of the event was not recorded. It was as if Jennifer's beautiful utterance was only meant for me: "fall . . . dive . . . many ways to fall . . . fall is multidirectional . . . more diving . . . multipolarity." The center image is *Seoul Spring* by Kwon Joo Hoon, May 20, 1986, courtesy of *Hankook Ilbo*. I first encountered it as I was browsing through Gwangju-related articles at the old Berlin State Library, Westhafen. I was in the states in 1986, studying art. It appears that I was a stupid girl then, oblivious to pain, and perhaps I still am. It appears that translation may have sensitized me to language at least. Now what? Translate, translate! Do it again, do it! Last year, even though she was ill, Kim Hyesoon kindly helped me to obtain the image from *Hankook Ilbo*. The photo on the right is *A man testing the wall*, courtesy of Federal Archives, Military Archives Division, Germany. I came upon the photo while walking along the remainder of the wall between East and West Germany at the Berlin Wall Memorial.

At the same time, I was tracing in my mind the dotted lines of the divided Korea (see *DMZ Colony*). It is estimated that it would take about a hundred years to completely demine, with over a million mines buried along the demilitarized zone. In the future, the former DMZ is safely demined by robots with the help of trained rats. Rats of the world unite against war, following the rat catcher in shorts. A permanent outdoor exhibition is built across the waist of a nation. A protected habitat for migratory birds as well as humans who must cross borders. Visitors at the 한반도통일미래센 터-Center for Unified Korean Future can enter the *Vessel of Peace* (by formalhaut—artists Gabriela Seifert and Götz Stöckmann) and look up and read a poem or look down at the water table that acts as a mirror. The Center for Sky Similes for Snow Geese holds regular international literary and translation programs. Helicopters drop poems from the sky: "return ... return ... return," "vowels forever," "Era uoy evila?" "oblong, oblong" and so on. The Museum of Clocks holds donated clocks from around the world, set to chime at all hours of grief. The Museum of Signs and Marks is still under construction. In the future, I return with my sister. We stand together under Mother's umbrella. Our future is not hollow.

"KWANGDSCHU": *Aktuelle Kamera*: Ereignisse in Kwangdschu vom 22.05.1980. Courtesy of Deutsches Rundfunkarchiv.

"Benjamin's Telephone": Heidi Broadhead gave me a copy of *One-Way Street*, translated by Edmund Jephcott (The Belknap Press of Harvard University Press, 2016), before I left for Berlin in 2019. Soon I saw Benjamin's memorial plaque near my apartment. It became a necessary part of my daily walk. "The Telephone," translated by Howard Eiland, is from *The Work of Art in the Age of Its Technological Reproducibility, and Other Writings on Media*, edited by Michael W. Jennings, Brigid Doherty, and Thomas Y. Levin (The Belknap Press of Harvard University Press, 2008).

"Ode S": The ring of Benz—I find myself, unconsciously or consciously, drawing a line straight down from one of the pointed ends. Peace is possible. The eye—one of many on the ceilings at the Berlin State Library that beam in light from the sky. Keats's quote is from "Ode to a Nightingale." Whenever I woke up in the middle of the night during my stay in Leipzig, October 2021 to March 2022, I listened to Sasha Dugdale's essay "An Ode to John Keats: Sasha Dugdale on 'Ode to a

Nightingale'" on BBC Sounds and fell back asleep. Lines in bold are from Virginia Woolf's *Mrs. Dalloway* (A Harvest/HBJ Book, 1985). I have always been struck by the presence of war in Woolf's writings. My sister and I with an umbrella by my father at Deoksugung Palace in Seoul. During my second visit to Gwangju in 2022 I obtained Lee Chang-seong's photograph of schoolchildren singing and protesting with their arms locked during the Gwangju Uprising. Courtesy of the May 18 Memorial Foundation. Arseny Tarkovsky's quote is from *Mirror* (1975) by Arseny Tarkovsky. The sparrow in *Mirror*, I thought, functioned as =. Of course, mirror, too. Sparrow = Mirror.

"IMPERIAL PANORAMA 1980": "Imperial Panorama" quotes are from *The Work of Art in the Age of Its Technological Reproducibility, and Other Writings on Media*. I was also informed and influenced by "Imperial Panorama: A Tour Through the German Inflation" in *One-Way Street*. "Critique of Violence" translated by Edmund Jephcott, is in Walter Benjamin, *Selected Writings: 1913–1926*, vol. 1.

From the State Berlin Library's East Asian Collection, I requested materials related to Gwangju. I was given a list of books, and *Indictment to the World: White Paper on Atrocious Kwangju Genocide* was included. The quotes from *Busan Ilbo* are in 5.18 광주민주화운동자료총서: 신문기자 자료모음집1. (A publication by the committee for compiling documents related to 5.18 Gwangju Uprising.) *Aktuelle Kamera* news scripts were kindly provided by Deutsches Rundfunkarchiv. "Miami Riot Continues" by Margot Hornblower and Merwin Sigale, © 1980 from the *Washington Post*. All rights reserved. Used under license.

I was informed by a *Dong-A Ilbo* archivist that my father held the copyright of the photo of my father and his mentor Paek Un-seon. My father sent me the photo a while back with a few others, including the photos of Taedong Bridge and Mekong Delta. He often included Post-it notes with the photos he mailed to me as if he were already preparing me for my future work.

"Mirror Nation": The photos of Sohn Kee-chung, the marathon runner of Berlin 1936, are courtesy of *Dong-A Ilbo*.

"Overlapping Marks": I traced in pencil all the watches and clocks on 9 pieces of tracing paper. The 3 scans are from the 3 sets of 3 overlapping tracing-paper pages. Kim Hyesoon told me when I was translating "I'm OK, I'm Pig!" (see *Sorrowtoothpaste Mirrorcream* and *Phantom Pain Wings*)

that she used the number 9 as a pig's tail. Sometimes, my translation and writing overlap as they

did in *Hardly War* and *DMZ Colony*. A form of "double-consciousness," in a way. These seemingly

meaningless marks helped me to synthesize Benjamin's notion of "temporal magic." For me

drawing is also about making and marking language.

"Swan Soliloquy": S / bridge leg with a swan at Eiserner Steg from my untitled 16 mm film, 1985.

"Frankfurt 1984": Eiserner Steg image and narration borrowed from the same 16 mm film. I filmed

it in December of 1984, then finished assembling the film with a voice-over. What I wrote might

have been a poem. Making films got me started in writing. My art professor Jeremy Gilbert-Rolfe

encouraged me to keep writing. But it's difficult to know why it took me this long to be able to

look at my film again. This transparent mark.

ACKNOWLEDGMENTS

My deep gratitude to Wave Books for making this trilogy a reality. I was able to send my manuscript in pieces to Joshua Beckman and Heidi Broadhead while certain parts of the book were still unfolding for me. This process enabled and motivated me to finish the book. I'm also grateful to the rest of the Wave team: Blyss Ervin, Catherine Bresner, Isabel Boutiette, Matthew Zapruder, and Charlie Wright. Admiration and gratitude to poet and book designer Jeff Clark.

Gratitude to Deborah Woodard, a poet and translator of Amelia Rosselli, for our enduring exchange, which has been an anchor for me, especially during the pandemic lockdown. To Richard Nicholls, my longtime colleague at Renton Technical College, for his insightful reading and encouragement. His father was a Kindertransport child. This makes Richard a child of a child of flight. We now share a deep connection to Sebald's work. To Sasha Dugdale and Kim Hyesoon for appearing in my thoughts and writing. To Tim Shorrock for his groundbreaking research and journalism on the Gwangju Uprising. To Srikanth Reddy for publishing my work in progress and for the conversation in *Poetry*'s special issue, *Exophony*. To Jennifer Kronovet for going to the Berlin State Library with me to listen and write. To Forrest Gander for visiting my childhood home. To Stephen Hong Sohn for *Minor Salvage: The Korean War and Korean American Life Writings* (University of Michigan Press, 2022).

I began working on *Mirror Nation* during my Berliner Künstlerprogramm des DAAD 2019 fellowship, which has profoundly reshaped my life: Thank you, Silvia Fehrmann, Laura Muñoz-Alonso, and Mathias Zeiske. The Picador Guest Professorship for Literature in 2021 enabled me to teach and have the time to write during my stay in Leipzig: Thank you, Friederike Busch and Vanessa Marzog.

The generous fellowships from the Guggenheim and MacArthur Foundations enabled me to travel for research and write freely. All the support I miraculously received will continue to sustain my future work.

As always, my work is created on behalf of my parents.